Phil H. LISTEMANN

Colour artwork: Claveworks Graphic

Layout & project design: Phil Listemann

Copyright © Philedition - Phil Listemann 2012

ISBN 978-2-918590-41-5

All rights reserved. No parts of this publication may be reproduced, stored in a retrieval system or transmitted in any form or by any means, electronic, mechanical, photocopying, recording or otherwise, without permission in writing from the Authors.

ACKNOWLEDGEMENTS

Phil Jarrett, Andrew Thomas, Roger Wallsgrove (Text Consultant)

Edited and printed by Phil H. Listemann

philedition@wanadoo.fr

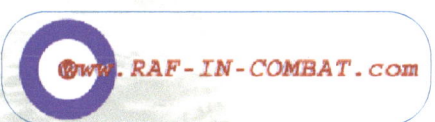

GLOSSARY OF TERMS

AC1: Aircraftman 1st Class
BER: Beyond Economical Repair
Cpl: Corporal
ECU: Experimental Co-operation Unit
F/L: Flight Lieutenant
F/O: Flying Officer
F/Sgt: Flight Sergeant
LAC: Leading Aircraftman

(NZ)/RAF: New Zealander serving with the RAF
P/O: Pilot Officer
RAF: Royal Air Force
Sgt: Sergeant
S/L: Squadron Leader
SOC: Struck of charge
Sqn: Squadron
W/C: Wing Commander

Short Singapore
INTRODUCTION

The first flying-boat named 'Singapore', N179, sailing slowly to its moorings. It was the only Singapore Mk.I built, not because it was a bad aircraft, but only because the Air Ministry had changed the specifications. *(Author's collection)*

The Short Singapore remained one of the most important seaplanes of the RAF of between the wars, even though built in small numbers, less than 40. For Shorts it was also crucial, representing almost half of their total production of flying-boats, military and civilian, in the 20 years after WW1.

The flying-boat emerged at the end of WWI as an essential tool for the British Empire to help to protect Britain's sea lanes and then the supply of advanced and high-performance seaplanes became a necessity. Short was not new in this market, having already built flying-boats during WWI, like the F.3 and F.5. After the war, the study of new designs continued, each time using new technology and in gathering all this experience and new technology, Short decided to respond to Specification 13/24, calling for an all-metal twin-engine flying-boat. This was to be based as far as Short is concerned on its "Cromarty", built in 1920-1921. The Short Singapore was born from that and received the serial N179. It was first flown on 17 August 1926. The Singapore I performed satisfactorily in the next few months and was chosen to be one of the four RAF flying-boats to make a tour of Baltic ports, which demonstrated the value of metal hulls. Despite this, no orders followed, mainly because the Air Ministry had issued in the meantime another Specification - R.32/27 - calling for long-range flying-boat to be powered by three engines, Bristol Jupiter radials or Rolls-Royce Kestrel in-lines. Having also built in the meantime the Short Calcutta for Imperial Airways, it was then logical for Short to use the Calcutta to respond to the new Specification. A prototype was ordered as the Singapore Mk.II and received the serial N246. Structurally, the Singapore II was similar to its predecessor, but better equipped internally for self-supporting operations away from base for lengthy periods. It made its maiden flight on 27 March 1930. The first trials led to Short, among other things, modifying the tail, and the single fin and rudder were changed for a triple tail unit, such as had already been adopted on the Blackburn Iris and Supermarine Southampton. Thus modified, the Singapore II flew for the first time on 17 February 1931 and started other tests including tropical trials at Aden. Upon its return to the UK, further modifications were made which included improved radiators and oil-coolers for the engines, a duralumin planing bottom on the hull and an enclosure over the pilot's cockpit. In this form, it flew on 6 May 1932, and with some more modifications added soon after, N246 had been brought virtually to the production standard that was defined by Specification R.3/33, against which the Air Ministry ordered four examples in August 1933. Thus, the Singapore Mk.III was finally born after many obstacles and changes of policy. They were serialled K3592 to K3595 and were delivered in July 1934 - 2 - and November the same year - 2 -. They had a crew of six. These four Singapores must be seen as pre-production aircraft as the following ones, 33, were all built against Specification R.14/34 which was issued for a fully developed production version with further up-rated Kestrels. Nine (K4577-4585) were later ordered in 1934, followed by 16 more in 1935 (K6907-6922), increased by four (K8856-8859) in 1936. All were delivered between April 1935 and June 1937.

The Singapore became the epitome of pre-war RAF flying-boats, and led to the Sunderland which played a major role during WW2 with Coastal Command and overseas.

Above, another view of N179, and its silhouette shows that this design was mid-way between the WW1 flying boats and the next generation to come. Note that N179 is shown here in its final form with Rolls-Royce H.10 Buzzard engines and Handley Page auto-slots on the upper wings. Note the name 'Singapore' written on the bow.
(Phil Jarrett)

Right N179 while used by Alan Cobham in civil guise as G-EBUP for a survey flight round Africa.
(Author's collection)

Below, the second Singapore, the four-engine N246 seen while taking off early in its career with a single tail as used by N179, and still with an open cockpit and no ailerons on the lower wings.
(Author's collection)

Singapore Mk.II was modified at various stages, starting with a new triple tail unit that was to become the hallmark of the Singapore Mk.III and ailerons on the lower wings (left). Afterwards, N246 was again modified by addition of a canopy over the pilot's cockpit and improved radiators for its Kestrel engines which were also adopted as standard for the Singapore III (above).
(Author's collection)

Below left, N246, moored at Mountbatten while on service trials with 210 Sqn in 1932. The Saro A.7 Severn, N240, also acquired for trials, can be seen in the background.
(Author's collection)

Deliveries and Strenght (RAF - Singapore III)

Month	Delivered	Total delivered	Acc.	SOC	On Hand
July 34	2	2	-	-	**2**
.../...					
November 34	2	4	-	-	**4**
.../...					
February 35	-	4	1	-	**3**
March 35	-	4	-	-	**3**
April 35	3	7	-	-	**6**
May 35	1	8	-	-	**7**
June 35	2	10	-	-	**9**
July 35	1	11	-	-	**10**
August 35	2	13	-	-	**12**
.../...					
January 36	2	15	-	-	**14**
February 36	1	16	-	-	**15**
March 36	2	18	1	-	**16**
April 36	-	18	-	-	**16**
May 36	1	19	-	-	**17**
June 36	1	20	-	-	**18**
July 36	3	23	-	-	**21**
August 36	1	24	-	-	**22**
September 36	1	25	-	-	**23**
October 36	1	26	-	-	**24**
November 36	2	28	-	-	**26**
December 36	1	29	-	-	**27**
January 37	2	31	-	-	**29**
February 37	2	33	1	-	**30**
March 37	1	34	-	-	**31**
April 37	2	36	-	-	**33**
May 37	-	36	-	-	**33**
June 37	1	37	-	-	**34**
July 37	-	37	-	-	**34**
August 37	-	37	1	-	**33**
September 37	-	37	1	-	**32**
.../...					
March 38	-	37	-	1	**31**
.../...					
July 38	-	37	-	1	**30**
.../...					
December 38	-	37	-	1	**29**
.../...					
March 39	-	37	1	-	**28**
April 39	-	37	-	-	**28**
May 39	-	37	1	-	**27**
June 39	-	37	-	-	**27**
July 39	-	37	2	1	**24**
August 39	-	37	1	3	**20**
September 39	-	37	-	1	**19**
.../...					
December 39	-	37	2	-	**17**
January 40	-	37	-	1	**16**
.../...					
March 40	-	37	-	1	**15**
April 40	-	37	-	-	**15**
May 40	-	37	-	1	**14**
.../...	-	37	-	-	**14**
August 40	-	37	-	1	**13**
.../...					
December 40	-	37	-	2	**11**
January 41					
February 41	-	37	-	1	**10**
.../...					
June 41	-	37	-	2	**8**
July 41	-	37	-	2	**6**
.../...					
October 41	-	37	-	4	**2**
December 41	-	37	-	1	**1**
.../...					
August 42	-	37	-	1	**-**

N246 taken from three-quarter front view at the end of its career. It is now very close to what the Singapore will be, and seen from a distance N246 can be easily mistaken for a Singapore III. *(Author's collection)*

TECHNICAL DATA
SHORT S.19 SINGAPORE MK.III

Manufacturer and production:
37 by Shorts

Type:
General reconnaissance flying-boat.

Accomodation:
Total of eight crew positions: pilot, co-pilot/navigator, one gunner/bomb-aimer in bows, one gunner in waist, one gunner in tail, one navigator, wireless operator, engineer.
(often reduced to six crewmen)

Power plant:
Two Rolls-Royce Kestrel VIII (aft) and two Kestrel XX (forward) six-cylinder water-cooled in-line engines each derated 610 hp.

Fuel & Oil
Fuel (Imp Gal):
Total (4 tanks): 1,266 [5 755 l]

Oil (Imp Gal):
Standard (4 tanks): 26.0 [118 l]
overload capacity: 42.0 [190.8 l]

Dimensions:
Span: 90 ft 0-in [30,48 m]
Length: 64 ft 2-in [19,56 m]
Height: 23 ft 6-in [7,16 m]
Wing area (upper and lower): 1,465 Sq ft [136,1 m²]

Weights:
Empty: 20,364 lb [9 237 kg]
Normal: 28,160 lb [12 773 kg]
Max overload: 32,390 lb [14 692 kg]

Performance:
Max cruising speed: 118 mph [190 km/h]

Economical cruising speed: 104 mph [167 km/h]

Service ceiling: 11,300 ft [3 444 m]
24,000 ft [7 300 m] for the F11C-2

Max range: 1,235 miles [1 987 km]

Endurance: 11.9 h at economical cruising speed

Armament:
Offensive:
max 2 x 550-lb bombs [250 kg] &
8 x 25-lb bombs [11.35 kg]

Defensive:
3 x 0.303-in [7.62 mm] in bow, waist and tail position

Two Short Singapores of 230 Sqn flying in pairs, K4578 coded 4 leading K4580 coded 1, shortly after their arrival at Alexandria (Egypt) in October 1935. This photo is not representative of the flights carried out by the Singapores, which used to fly alone. (*Author's collection*)

No.210 Squadron
Code: nil
November 1934 - November 1938

The first unit to receive the new RAF flying-boat was 210 Sqn based at Pembroke Dock. It was equipped with the Supermarine Southampton II. 210 Sqn was thus selected to conduct service trials and operational training with the three pre-production Singapore Mk.IIIs (K3592-3595) in 1934. Except for K3592, all were taken on squadron charge shortly after delivery to the RAF, K3592 being first used by the MAEE and joined the squadron after four months of trials. Once the first crews were trained, the four Singapores were sent to their overseas stations and the ferry flights were carried out in mid-January 1935. All Singapores reached their destination, Singapore - rather appropriate for this case! - in April, all but one, K3595 captained by Flight Lieutenant H.L. Beatty, did not make it as it crashed into a hill in bad weather near Messina in Sicily on 15 February 1935. There were no survivors among the nine crewmen, including Mr. Reginald J.P. from RAE Farnborough who was flying as passenger.

Replacement of these four pre-production Singapores came in April with the arrival of the 'true' Singapores with the same purpose, train crews for the other squadrons. Hence, K4578 was the first to arrive followed by K4582 in June, K4583 in July, K4584 in August, but once again all had left for their respective units by Autumn that year. In September 1935 due to the Abbysinian crisis (invasion of Ethiopia by Italy), the squadron was temporary equipped with Rangoons and sent to Gibraltar, returning in August 1936 to re-equip with Singapores, this time to become a true operational unit. When the production of the Singapore had come to an end, the squadron was using the following Singapores: K6920, K6565, K8566, K8568, K8858, K8859 (the last Singapore built), the number of aircraft on charge being the normal complement of an operational flying-boat squadron at that time. In September 1937, the squadron was detached to Algeria as part of an Anglo-French force assembled to counter the activities of submarines attacking neutral shipping during the Spanish Civil war and returned to the UK in December. 1938 remained uneventful for the Singapores which finally left the squadron in November that year after 210 Sqn had been totally converted to the Short Sunderland. During most of this period, the CO of 210 Sqn had been W/C W.N. Plenderleith. The first squadron really selected to operate the

No.205 Squadron
Code: FV
April 1935 - October 1941

The first squadron really selected to operate the Singapore was 205 Sqn based at Seletar (Singapore). The first three aircraft made the journey in January 1935 arriving in April (less K3535, see above). These three Singapores served in the next few months and never returned to the UK. All were struck off charge by 1938, two (K3592 and K3593) as time-expired, the last one, K3594, after being lost in accident at night on 2 February 1937. That night, with S/L A.W. Bates in command, K3594 was taking off from the Jahore Straits for a night combined operations search patrol when the flying-boat swung on take-off to avoid running aground and a wing dug in. The Singapore cra-

The Short Singapore served with 205 Sqn in Singapore until a few weeks before the Japanese attack in December 1941. One is seen in the background with its successor, the Consolidated Catalina, of which three can be seen in this hangar. The one in the foreground has the squadron code FV-T painted in full in an unusual location, the tail. (*Author's collection*)

shed, causing the death of one airman, Pilot Officer Robert D. Blair. Meanwhile, the squadron had received reinforcements with the arrival of K4581 in August 1935, K6910 in May 1936. K4581 was also struck off charge at the same time as the three pre-production Singapores became time-expired, and 205 Sqn continued to be operational with K6910, K6911 and K6916. When the British Empire entered into war in September 1939 things remained unchanged, except for a new CO W/C A.F. Lang who arrived in October. Located far from the danger, as Japan wasn't a threat yet, the activities of the squadron didn't change a lot in the first weeks of the war. However, the squadron received reinforcements with the arrival in spring 1940 of three other Singapores, K6912, K6917 and K6918, and squadron codes 'FV' made their appearance on the fuselage. Some air reconnaissance flights were carried out in November 1939, mainly to locate possible German raiders. Indeed London had asked the squadron to find and locate any German merchant vessels sailing in the area and three Singapores were not enough to conduct the operations with success. Thus April 1940 saw a sudden increase of air activity, which reduced the following month but increased again after the 10th June when Italy declared war and the squadron had to locate Italians merchant vessels, as then activity reduced again in July. Nevertheless, operational activity remained at a very low level in 1939-1940 as only 30 sorties, which include some ASR missions, could be recorded for a total of 175 operational flying hours. In 1941, the situation had begun to change in the region and it had become clear that Japan would enter into war soon. By that time, 205 Sqn was the last RAF operator of the Singapore, which was totally obsolete in 1940 and with airframe hours of some aircraft close to being time-expired or actually time-expired like K6910, which had been struck off charge in May 1940. But the Air Ministry had already found its successor, as the Consolidated Catalina began to arrive at Seletar in April 1941. From that moment onwards, the Singapores flew less and in October 1941, four of them (K6912, K6916, K6917 and K6918) were passed on to the RNZAF which needed general reconnaissance aircraft to be based at Fiji. It is not sure if the last Singapore still on squadron charge, K6911, continued to fly after that date, but it was officially struck off charge on 11 December, three days after the beginning of the war in South East Asia.

No.203 Squadron
Code: NT
September 1935 - February 1940

Based at Basra (Iraq) shortly after its formation in January 1929, 203 Sqn operated Supermarine Southamptons and Short Rangoons before being selected to receive Singapores. Conversion began in September 1935 with the arrival of K4582 and K4583 on 24 September, while at the same time the squadron moved to Aden (Isthmus) due to the invasion of Ethiopia by Mussolini's troops. By the end of the year, two other Singapores were taken on charge (K4577 and K4584) to make the full complement of four. At Aden, the main task was to fly submarine co-operation sorties as well as transporting mail. In July 1936, the squadron returned to Basra to continue more routine flights. In September, K4582 was sent to the UK and left Basra on 15th. Seven days later, while doing the leg between Brindisi (Italy) and Berre in France, the flying boat flown by F/L R.S. Darbyshire was caught in a storm and was obliged to make a force-landing at Paolo near Cosenza in Italy. If no injuries were reported by the crew, the Singapore could not be saved and was broken up by waves. It was eventually sold for scrap locally the

following month. When war broke out the squadron moved to its war station at Aden and began anti-shipping patrols and escort works. This task began with reduced resources as two Sinpapores had been lost early in the year, starting with K6908 on 14 March. That day, with S/L M.Q. Candler in command, the Singapore swung while taxying and ran aground. The flying-boat was repairable but due to the high airframe hours (over 700 hours), it was decided not to conduct repairs and the aircraft was struck off charge in May. More dramatically, three weeks before the beginning of the war, 203 Sqn lost another Singapore when, on take-off from Aboukir 8 August 1939, K4584 captained by S/L James R. Scarlett-Streatfield hit a sea wall and crashed. Among the crew, three died either the same day, or the following day, but it had been a severe blow for the squadron just before war broke out. This did not prevent the squadron from beginning operation and on the 4th September, Flying Officer S.C. Pendred took off at 03.40 GMT with his crew for the first operational patrol of the war for a Singapore, followed two hours later by K6907 captained by F/O J.M.N. Pike. In September, the number of sorties rose to 22, but soon after reduced to a handful per month when it became obvious the area would not be affected by war for a short while. It was more sad knowing the squadron was actually living its last days as a flying boat squadron and before the end of the year, Blenheims began to arrive for conversion on type, while in the same time Singapores continued to fly anti-submarine patrols. The last of these was carried out by F/L J.M.N. Pike with K6907 on 10 February 1940. When he landed at 20.00 that day, the squadron had performed about 50 sorties since September for 280 hours of patrol. From this moment, only 205 Sqn in Singapore remained operational on Singapores.

No.230 Squadron
Code: Nil
April 1935 - November 1938

230 Sqn was the next to follow. Starting with K4579, the squadron began to receive its full allotment in April 1935. It was flown from the manufacturers to Pembroke Dock on the 26th. K4578 and K4580 followed in June, K4581 in July and K4585 in August and by then the squadron had its full complement of four. In September, 230 Sqn received orders that it was to proceed to the Middle East. The reason was for this haste was the 'Abyssinian crisis' which arose at that time. Based at Alexandria, the Singapores began to undertake patrols checking on Italian shipping movements. Only one major event has to recorded for this period when K4579 caught fire starting up and the aircraft was saved from total destruction owing to the prompt action made by Flying Officer Pettit and Corporal Berryman, who saved the Singapore from the fire. After one year of operations, the squadron returned to the UK. The return journey came close to creating a major diplomatic issue, however, when K6912 flown by Flying Officers Oliver and Wills had to force land off Vigo in Spain, where the Civil War had begun! However, the problem could be solved as the crew were able to keep the engines running to avoid approaching too close to the Spanish coast. A Spanish rowing boat approached but could not come alongside as K6912 was being guarded by K4580 (flown by the CO, W/C W.H. Dunn, who remained the CO during most of the Singapore era) which had landed alongside. After provisional repairs, both Singapores were able to complete the trip back. The squadron remained then a short time in the UK and in October departed Pembroke Dock for Singapore and stayed in Asia until the Short

After the Munich crisis, the RAF began to camouflage its aircraft, including flying boats, and assigned squadron codes letters. 203 Sqn stationed at Basra (Iraq) was assigned the letters 'NT'. *(Andrew Thomas)*

Various scenes of the mechanics undergoing maintenance of 203 Sqn Singapores, proving that the mechanics had to have more than the usual mechanical skills to do their job, flexibility and balance! *(Phil Jarrett)*

Singapore Mark IIIs, including K8567 'M' and K8566 'B', of 230 Squadron, being loaded onto HMS Cyclops from a jetty at Arzeu, Algeria, 1936. *(Phil Jarrett)*

Sunderland began to arrive in June 1938, 230 Sqn Singapores being passed on to 205 Sqn.

No.209 Squadron
Code: nil
February 1936 - December 1938

209 Sqn, based at Felixtowe and under the command of W/C C.R. Cox, received its first Singapore, K6909, on 13 February 1936. However, the squadron had to wait until November to have its full complement of four. The squadron's task was to cover the Western Approaches and the English Channel. In 1937, under the command of W/C G.W. Bentley, the squadron flew a cruise to Malta and it also co-operated with radio and radar experiments with RAF Bawdsey. Later that year it moved to Malta for anti-piracy and anti-submarine patrols, only returning from the Mediterranean at the end of the year to begin conversion onto the Stranraer. The last Singapore left the unit in December making an end to an uneventful two and a half years of use.

No.240 Squadron
Code: nil
November 1938 - July 1939

This was the last squadron to be equipped with Singapores. Reformed in March 1937 by expanding C Flight, Seaplane Training Squadron (STS) up to full strength, it was originally equipped with Supermarine Scapas. However despite this, it continued to work as a training unit until being re-equipped with Singapores in November 1938, becoming operational on 1 January 1939 under No.16 (Coastal) Group authority with K6920, K8566 and K8568 at Calshot, S/L M.W.C. Ridgway being the CO. In the next few weeks, other Singapores came to reinforce the squadron. If the operational use of the Singapore was short, about six months, 240 Sqn recorded some major accidents during this short period of time. The first of these occurred on 15 May 1939 when K8568, flown by F/L A.A. de Gruyther while returning from a training flight, hit the ground while descending out of cloud and force-landed at Felixstowe with a badly damaged hull. No injuries were reported to the crew but as the Singapores were at the end of their service life, it was not repaired. On 6 July 1939, it was the turn of K6920 to be wrecked. While taking off for a conversion flight, the wing dropped and a float was torn off. Nobody on board was hurt, including the pilot, P/O Wilfrith P. Green who had only 6 hours logged on type, but the aircraft was eventually struck off charge in September for the same reasons as K8568. Despite this Green flew throughout the war, being awarded the DSO, until he was killed in March 1945 as CO of 219 Sqn. Bad luck continued for 240 Sqn as, nine days later, P/O Dennis S.M. Burrell, with only four hours on the type, did not control completely the Singapore's swing on take-off for a conversion flight and hit the mast of a steamer, which damaged the aircraft. It was struck off charge before the war broke out. Burrell was not lucky either as he was killed the following September while serving with 269 Sqn, attacking a German flying-boat off Norway at the control of his Anson. However these bad times had come to an end as fortunately the Saro London had begun to arrive at the squadron and the Singapores left before the end of July.

Two Singapores of 209 Sqn flying in loose formation approaching Felixstowe in 1938, K6914/C leading, followed by K6914/M. Actually this photo was taken from a third Singapore K6919/Y (see p.25). *(Phil Jarrett)*

Singapore K6912 OT-A taken shortly after take-off a while after the introduction of the type in the RNZAF inventory. This aircraft performed the first operational flight from Fiji on 6 January 1942. *(Author's collection)*

No.5 Squadron, RNZAF
Code: OT
November 1941 - April 1943

With Japanese intentions in Asia and the Pacific becoming increasingly aggressive, the small Royal New Zealand Air Force had an urgent requirement for a flying-boat to fulfil its patrol responsibilities in the South Pacific. Modern equipment like the Catalina was in short supply and so the RNZAF was offered some second-hand Singapores previously used by 205 Sqn based in Singapore. Although the type was obsolescent, the Singapores were seen as stop-gap waiting for more modern aircraft and the offer was accepted. Four aircraft, K6912, K6916, K6917 and K6918 were allocated. Even though rather close to their time-expired airframe hours, the number of hours still to be flown were considered as enough before the time came to receive more modern and potent flying boats.

Before using the Singapores at the planned base at Fiji, the flying boats had to be collected. The RNZAF personnel, under the responsibility of S/L E.M. Lewis, arrived at Seletar in September 1941 for this purpose. The New Zealanders were firstly trained on the type by 205 Sqn personnel, and by mid-October, the first two Singapores were ready to make the long ferry flight to Fiji. The four flying boats were officially transferred to the RNZAF on 14th and two days later, K6916 and K6917 and their crews lifted off from Seletar.

To operate the four Singapores, a squadron was raised, No.5 Sqn, RNZAF, which was officially formed on 18 November 1941, S/L Lewis becoming its first CO. With tensions in South East Asia rising, on 1 December the second ferry flight in Singapore under S/L B.W Baird was placed at the disposal of HQ Far East and attached logically to 205 Sqn. The Japanese landed on the Malay peninsula seven days later and during the day, the Singapores flew uneventful operational patrols. On the 10th they gave reconnaissance support to *Force Z* (HMS *Prince of Wales* and HMS *Repulse*), but had returned to base before the vessels were attacked and sunk later in the day. After these two missions, the aircraft completed preparations at Seletar and left on

Group. Original crew of RNZAF Short Singapore K6917. L-R: E Taylor, rigger. J Winefield, navigator. W Burgess, pilot. M Harman, radio operator. W Alcock, rigger. Front: K Kennedy, engineer. S Smart, engineer. Fiji, possibly Suva. Circa late 1941.

Group. Original crew of RNZAF Short Singapore K6916. L-R: E Stukey, rigger. E Lewis, pilot. O Hickson, navigator. W Stringer, radio operator. Front; F Hughes, rigger. W Taylor, engineer. R Gibbs, engineer. Fiji, possibly Suva. Circa late 1941.

Above and below one of the No.5 Sqn Singapores while under maintenance, which was also carried out by local people. Note that one crewman is adding some black paint on the hull. It is not known exactly when this Singapore received this new paint and if all were treated like this. The Singapores received also an unofficial insignia which could not be detailed with certainty, but was constituted of the numeral '5' with a bird and an inscription below. (*Author's collection*)

Singapore K6917 being pushed into the water to carry out another patrol. Fortunately for the Kiwi crews, the area was free of any Japanese fighters, otherwise the Singapore had little chance to escape and was an easy prey to any fighters in 1942. *(Author's collection)*

the long journey to Fiji on 13 December.

In Fiji, serious operations began on 15 December when S/L Lewis flew a survey sortie in K6916 to examine proposed RDF (navigation aid) sites. However, the career of K6916 with the RZNAF was short as two days later during a take-off from Suva for a trip to Nandi, a creeping elevator trim became evident and the take-off was aborted. Unfortunately the Singapore overran the surveyed alighting area and ran onto a mud bank and was severely damaged. Considering its age and the small number of spare parts and lack of facilities to undertake repairs, K6916 was declared as beyond economical repair and written off in July 1942. During the month, the size of the squadron continued to be extended with arrival of more personnel and by the end of December, the squadron could be considered as totally operational with three Singapores, as the last two had arrived in the meantime from Seletar.

5 Sqn's main task was anti-submarine patrols, with convoy escorts and surface surveillance to shadow any possible Japanese surface raiders. It was also tasked with communications flights between the various islands and atolls. The first operational flight was carried out on 6 January 1942 when K6912/OT-A flown by F/L MacGergor flew an anti-submarine patrol. In the next few weeks, the flights were regularly scheduled but due to the small number of planes and spares, the overall operational activity remained low, with 12 sorties in January, 15 in February and 16 in March. The routine continued during the next two months with an average of 20 sorties monthly. The squadron was added a Vickers Vincent flight on 27 May and became officially an Army Co-operation unit, but that didn't change anything for the Singapore crews. On 10 July, F/L MacGregor and crew in K6912/OT-A provided an anti-submarine escort for the departure of the SS '*Thomas Jefferson*' from Suva. The crew was not long airborne before sighting a surfaced submarine and attacked it, dropping a single 250-lb bomb on the rapidly submerging vessel. It was seen to go down vertically and was claimed as damaged. That became the only claim ever by a Short Singapore during the war.

At this time, the Japanese had advanced deep into the South Pacific, even appeared to threaten Fiji and consequently, maritime reconnaissance in the area needed to be increased in importance. However, the number of Singapores and their availability did not permit this, and the arrival of USN squadron VP-11 on Catalinas in Fiji was particularly welcomed. The former designation 'Bomber Reconnaissance' of the squadron was restored during the summer and when the unit moved to the newly-completed base at Lauthala Bay in September 1942, but by that time, the Singapores were in decline with problems owing to age and shortage of spare parts. That month, the Singapores were able to carry out 23 sorties, but that became the swansong the flying boat as operational activity decreased dramatically in October. It was slightly increased in November but all operational activity ceased on 23 November when F/O McHardy and crew performed the last anti-submarine patrol with K6918/OT-D. Four days later, a last flight was recorded with K6918 with F/L MacGregor in command, and the squadron formally disbanded on 22 January 1943. However, due to unforeseen problems with deployment of RNZAF Catalinas in Fiji, the Singapore Flying Boat Flight was formed under the now S/L MacGregor at Lauthala Bay late February 1943 with two Singapores, K6912 and K6918, K6917 having being withdrawn from use to provide spares for the other two. It was only an interim measure pending the arrival of 6 Sqn, RNZAF with its Catalinas. Operations began on 2 March and during the next six weeks, 22 more sorties were carried out, the last being recorded on 16 April 1943. But maintenance became day after day more difficult to undertake, due to various major technical problems and chronic shortage of spares, then forced their definitive withdrawal. The last two Singapores were eventually scuttled, making an end to an unexpectedly long life and history of the Singapores with the RNZAF. In all these four Singapores carried out about 175 operational sorties, representing almost 1,000 operational hours with about more 400 hours of training and various flights to be added to this tally, rather high considering the age of this flying boat and the various problems encountered during its service life with the RZNAF. The Short

Second-line and miscellaneous units

Singapore was used by a few second-line or miscellaneous units. 228 Sqn was among them, even being a true operational squadron, its connection with the Singapore was marginal. Indeed, 228 Sqn was re-formed as a flying-boat squadron and was intended for the new Supermarine Stranraer, based at Pembroke Dock. However, the aircraft was not fully ready and the squadron had to be equipped with various spare aircraft including Singapores. Actually only three Singapores were taken on squadron charge: K4579 between March and September 1937, K6913 between May and October 1937 and K8856 between March and July 1937. By autumn things reverted to normal, and the Stranraer had become the regular equipment of the squadron and the presence of the Singapores had become unnecessary.

If we exclude the use of three Singapores (K4578, K4580, K8565) by D Flight MAEE, formally Experimental Co-operation unit (ECU), between September 1938 and September 1939, the Singapore was principally flown by a single second-line unit, the Flying Boat Training Squadron (FBTS). Formed on 2 January 1939 at Calshot in No.14 Group, it took progressively the training role of 240 Sqn and was equipped with various flying-boats including Singapore IIIs. Its role was to train flying boat pilots. The Singapores were sent to Calshot for FBTS use early in 1939 and with the withdrawal of the Singapore from front line units, more became available and by October 1939, K4578, K4579, K4580, K8865, K8856 were used to train pilots at FBTS. As with many training units, the training was not carried out without incidents, and two occurred in December 1939. The first of these involved K8856 which stalled from 20 feet in landing off Hillhead (Hants). The pilot, P/O W. Berringer didn't have a lot of experience and had only flown six hours on the type and the flying instructor didn't have time to recover. The hull was damaged but seemed to be repairable but sank under tow. It was written off the following month. One week later, bad luck again hit the FBTS when P/O A.J. Bradley, while taxying K4580 off Calshot for a practice solo flight, collided with Lerwick L7250 at moorings. Investigation took time but considering the near withdrawal of the type, K4580 was struck off charge in October 1940. To make up attrition K6909 arrived in December 1939. Except for the loss of K6909 which sank during a gale on 22 August 1940, things continued without other major incident until March 1941 when FBTS became the nucleus of No.4 (C) OTU. At that time, only K4579, K6922, K8565 and K8567 remained in the inventory, soon joined by K4578. However the days of the Singapores were already numbered and before June was gone, the Singapores had left the OTU being replaced by more modern flying boats.

The Short Singapore, if it didn't played a major role during WW2 with only about 230 sorties and over 1,300 operational hours, was the necessary step for Shorts to lead to the Sunderland which played a major role during the Battle of the Atlantic and overseas.

Singapore K6917 under major overhaul at an unspecific date, unless it was at the time it was serving as stock of spare parts for K6912 and K6918 as it became in 1943. *(Author's collection)*

THE REGISTER

Four Short Singapore IIIs ordered by contract 244794/33

K3592

First flight 16.06.34, MAEE 21.07.34 for performance trials; damaged on slipway due to bad trolley design, Felixtowe, 13.10.34; repaired; No.210 Sqn 30.11.34; Singapore Delivery Flight 15.01.35; No.205 Sqn 02.04.35. SOC 27.12.37 as time-expired [718.5 TT].

Singapore K3592 seen at various stages of its trials at MAEE in 1934-1935 without any particular markings. (*Author's collection*)

Take-off of K3592 seen from a different angle. Without a doubt, the Singapore easily gives the feeling of power combined with elegance. In 1934, the Singapore is however one of the biggest military flying-boat flying of the World. (*Author's collection*)

Below, K3592 now being operated by an operational squadron, 205 Sqn located at Singapore. It first carried Clubs markings. The four allocated Singapores applied the symbols of the four card suits as individual identification. (*Author's collection*)

K3593

FF 24.07.34; damaged 30.07.34 and repaired at Works; No.210 Sqn 31.07.34 for service trials; Singapore Delivery Flight 15.01.35; No.205 Sqn 02.04.35. SOC 30.03.38 [541.7 TT].

At first sight, this photo of K3593 doesn't bring much interest and was probably taken early in its career. However, the presence of a Seahorse below the cockpit suggests that K3593 was used by 203 Sqn (the seahorse being the symbol of this unit's crest), something that never officially occurred. The presence of such a drawing is not explained, and might be only provisional and applied during the ferry flight to the Far East for delivery to 205 Sqn while making a stop-over in the Middle East where 203 Sqn was stationed.
Below, the same aircraft while serving in Singapore with 205 Sqn with a black Spade painted under the cockpit, the first individual markings applied to K3593. It was painted on both sides.
(Both - Author's collection)

Above, the same aircraft ashore for maintenance now coded '3', the last code K3593 used before being withdrawn from use in 1938. (*Author's collection*)

K3594
Del No.210 Sqn 06.11.34; Singapore Delivery Flight 15.01.35; No.205 Sqn 02.04.35. Swung to avoid running aground on night take-off and wing dug in, Johore Straits (Seletar) 02.02.37. SOC 15.08.37 [567.8 TT].

K3594 seen at various moments while serving 205 Sqn in the Far East. First with Hearts markings under the cockpit, later changed for a number '7' then '4' with which it was lost in an accident in February 1937 taking the life of one crewman. (*Author's collection*)

K3595
Delivered No.210 Sqn 13.11.34; Singapore Delivery Flight 15.01.35; Crashed into mountains in bad weather near Messina, Sicily (Italy) 15.02.35. SOC 03.12.35.

Nine Short Singapore IIIs delivered by contract 330930/34

K4577
Delivered Felixtowe 05.04.35 for armament and equipment trials; No.209 Sqn 18.09.35, left for Aden 30.09.35; No.203 Sqn 10.10.35; hit rock taxying and beached, Um Rasas 06.04.38 - repaired. SOC 03.01.40 and moored out as decoy June 1940.

K4578
Delivered No.210 Sqn 11.04.35; Shorts 31.03.35; No.230 Sqn 22.06.35; No.228 Sqn 12.07.37; No.210 Sqn 20.09.37; ECU 27.09.38, FBTS 01.09.39; No.4 OTU 05.06.41. SOC 31.08.42.

K4578 of 210 Sqn while being lifted out of the water. It was allocated the letter 'F'. Its service with 210 Sqn was short, a one year period. (*Author's collection*)

K4579
Delivered No.230 Sqn 26.04.35; caught fire starting up 24.06.36 - repaired; returned to the UK 13.08.36; No.210 Sqn date unrecorded; No.228 Sqn 22.03.37; Shorts 27.09.37; No.209 Sqn 19.07.38; No.240 Sqn 11.05.39; FBTS 11.06.39; No.4 OTU 16.03.41. SOC 07.05.41.

K4580
Delivered No.230 Sqn 21.05.35; No.210 Sqn date unrecorded; Shorts 28.02.38; No.209 Sqn 16.09.38; ECU 07.10.38; FBTS 06.09.39. Collided with Lerwick L7250 taxying off Calshot, 12.12.39. SOC 14.10.40.

K4581
Delivered No.230 Sqn 05.06.35; No.205 Sqn 30.08.35. SOC 22.03.38 as time-expired. [711.0 TT]

K4581 seen at Plymouth in June or July 1935 while under 210 Sqn authority before being ferried out by a crew of this unit.
(*Author's collection*)

Singapore K4581 seen at Aboukir bay during summer 1935 while in transit for delivery to 205 Sqn.
(*Phil Jarrett*)

The same flying-boat taken sometime after its arrival in Singapore. It has yet to have its individual number '1' painted on. It was eventually withdrawn from use with 711 airframe hours, a rather low total time for an aircraft of this category
(*Author's collection*)

This photo of K4582 is believed to have been taken during the ferry flight to Iraq for service with 203 Sqn, as no specific markings can be noticed on this Singapore at its moorings. If so, it could have been taken in September 1935. (*Phil Jarrett*)

K4582

Delivered No.210 Sqn 29.06.35. Left for ferry flight to Iraq 09.09.35; No.203 Sqn 24.09.35. Returned to the UK 15.09.37. Forcelanded in storm Paolo, Cosenza, Italy 22.09.37. Broken up by waves and sold for scrap locally 04.10.37. [593 TT].

Embarrassing situation for K4582 while serving with 203 sqn at Aden. Nothing is known about the circumstances which obliged the pilot to make a force-landing on the sand. This incident is even not written on its movement card, but it is sure is that it was able to be repaired to flying condition. However, the next time, returning to the UK, it would run of luck and was unable to complete the journey, which was stopped in Italy. (*Author's collection*)

K4583
Delivered No.210 Sqn 09.07.35. Left on ferry flight to Iraq 09.09.35; No.203 Sqn 24.09.35; No.210 Sqn 17.12.37; Shorts 01.05.38; SOC 15.07.38 as BER.

Left, K4583 at moorings at an unknown location, but probably in the UK, just before leaving for Aden and logically in service with 210 Sqn. Note once again the lack of markings which reinforces that idea. Right, if not impressive, this photo is very interesting because it shows the undersurfaces, and how the black parts were painted. It also shows also the serials and how they were written. (*Phil Jarrett*)

K4584
Delivered No.210 Sqn 10.08.35; Left on ferry flight to Iraq 09.09.35. Tail damaged on take-off, Gibraltar 12.09.35 - repaired. No.203 Sqn 07.10.35. Left for Uk 15.09.37; No.228 Sqn 09.10.37; Shorts 05.11.37; No.210 Sqn 21.05.38; No.203 Sqn 03.06.38; wing hit-sea on landing in glassy calm, Khor Jarama, 31.07.38 - repaired. Hit sea wall on take off, Aboukir 08.08.39. Destroyed by fire. SOC 15.07.40 [846.8 TT]

K4585
Delivered No.230 Sqn 30.08.35. SOC 12.12.38 [713.8 TT]

Sixteen Short Singapores IIIs delivered against contract 396872/35

K6907
Delivered to Calshot 02.01.36; Left on ferry flight to Aden 16.01.36; No.203 Sqn 30.01.36. SOC 23.03.40 and moored out at Aden as decoy.

K6908
Delivered to Calshot 17.01.36. Left on ferry flight to Aden date unrecorded. No.203 Sqn 17.02.36; drifted on to submerged rock, Merbat, 20.02.38; salvaged and repaired. Swung while taxying and ran aground, Margil, 14.03.39. SOC 20.05.39 as BER.

K6909
Delivered No.209 Sqn 13.02.36; No.240 Sqn 20.03.39; FBTS 15.12.39. Sank in gale, Stranraer 22.08.40. SOC 28.09.40.

K6910
Delivered MAEE 06.03.36; No.205 Sqn 22.05.36. SOC 31.05.40 (probably as time-expired).

K6911
Delivered MAEE 12.03.36; collided with yacht while taxying, Rochester 30.03.36 - repaired 14.04.36. No.205 Sqn 22.05.36. SOC 11.12.41.

Below, K6910 coded '5' flying over the Malayan countryside whilst serving with 205 Sqn in Singapore. Later, with the introduction of codes, it was allocated the code FV-F. It was SOC on 31.05.40, but for unknown reasons, either because it had reached its airframe limit or following a minor accident and not repaired, to be converted to spares to supply other Singapores still in service, knowing that spares parts were a recurrent problem for the aircraft in Singapore. (*Author's collection*) The quality is far from excellent, but this photo is interesting showing K6912 during 230 Sqn's journey to the Far East which began in October 1936. K6912 was eventually camouflaged and coded NT-D (see p.10) and later served with 205 Sqn as FV-F and was eventually transferred to the RNZAF in October 1941 and coded OT-A - see next page - top. (*Andrew Thomas*)

K6912 was transferred to the RNZAF in October 1941 and coded OT-A. (*Author's collection*)
K6913 taken in flight during a routine patrol while in service with 203 Sqn in Basra (Iraq). Note the black paint covering most of the undersurfaces. (*Author's collection*)

K6912
Delivered Felixstowe 22.05.36; No.230 Sqn 03.08.36. No.203 Sqn 29.09.38. Left Aden to Singapore 07.05.40; No.205 Sqn 15.05.40. To RNZAF 14.10.41. Damaged in an accident 17.12.41. SOC July 1942.

K6913
Delivered No.209 Sqn 11.06.36; No.228 Sqn 20.05.37; left for Iraq 19.10.37; No.203 Sqn 03.11.37; moored out at decoy at Aden June 1940. SOC 20.12.40.

K6914
Delivered No.209 Sqn 01.07.36; SOC 23.08.39

K6915
Delivered No.209 Sqn 16.07.36. SOC 23.08.39.

K6916
Delivered No.210 Sqn 31.07.36; No.230 Sqn 17.09.36; No.205 Sqn 29.06.38. To RNZAF 14.10.41 - No.5 Sqn; Damaged in accident 15.12.41. BER and SOC July 1942.

K6917
Delivered No.210 Sqn 27.08.36; No.209 Sqn 19.09.36; No.230 Sqn 13.11.36; No.205 sqn 01.05.38; To RNZAF 14.10.41 - No.5 Sqn. SOC April 1943.

The Short Singapore was totally obsolete when the British Empire entered into war against Japan in 1941. The Singapore was a stop-gap waiting for more modern aircraft, but because the war against the Japanese changed priorities regarding the delivery of aircraft, the New Zealanders had to operate Singapores for longer than planned. Fortunately the area the Singapores had to fly over was not an area frequented by the Japanese, because the Singapore had little chance to survive. Below K6917/OT-C of No.5 Sqn, RNZAF had just taken off for another patrol from the Fijis. (*Author's collection*)

K6918 of 205 Sqn which had recently received camouflage and a full combination of codes, FV-L. It was later transferred to the RNZAF as OT-D. (*Author's collection*)

K6918
Delivered No.230 Sqn 07.09.36; No.205 Sqn 23.07.38; To RNZAF 14.10.41 - No.5 sqn. SOC April 1943.

K6919
Delivered No.209 Sqn 22.10.36; No.240 Sqn 07.07.39. SOC 19.07.39.

K6919 served with 209 Sqn during its career and wore the letter code 'Y'. It is seen flying in astern formation, being the last of the line, probably for display or a ferry flight as the Singapores had no operational tactics requiring such flights. Note the upper wings have been repaired and the mechanics have still to repaint the roundel which has been partially cut. (*Phil Jarrett*)

Later on, it served for a very short time with 240 Sqn, less than two weeks in July 1939, but was probably unused by the squadron. K6919 is seen here down on the shore, partially scrapped and lightened of some of its components like the engines and propellers, making us assume that it was serving as spare parts stock for the other Singapores of the fleet. (*Author's collection*)

K6920

Delivered No.210 Sqn 13.11.36; Shorts 06.10.37; No.210 Sqn 19.10.37; No.240 sqn 22.11.38; Wing dropped on take-off and float torn off, Calshot 06.07.39. SOC as BER.

K6921

Delivered No.209 Sqn 30.11.36. SOC 23.08.39.

Singapore K6921 'Z', of 209 Squadron, setting out from Mountbatten for anti-piracy patrols in the Mediterranean, 18 September 1937. The Singapores were based at Kalafrana (Malta) for three months before returning to the UK. (*Author's collection*)

Once withdrawn from front line units, the Singapore helped the new Coastal Command crews to be trained and qualified on flying-boats, a task the Flying-Boats Training squadron (FBTS) had inherited from 240 Sqn at the outbreak of war. The denomination was later changed to No.4 OTU. Here, K8585 coded 'Q' taken during a training flight during winter 1940-1941. K8565 is wearing the standard camouflage of that period - see colour profile -. (*Author's collection*)

K6922

Delivered MAEE 04.12.36; No.240 Sqn 24.06.39; FBTS 24.09.39; No.4 OTU 16.03.41. SOC 03.06.41 [402.1 TT]

Four Singapore IIIs delivered to contract 396872/35

K8565

delivered No.210 Sqn 02.01.37; No.209 Sqn 13.08.38; ECU 02.09.38; FBTS 06.09.39 then No.4 OTU 16.03.41. SOC 30.06.41.

K8566

Delivered No.210 Sqn 16.01.37; No.240 Sqn 07.11.38. Swung on take-off and hit mast of steamer, Calshot 15.07.39. SOC 28.09.39 as BER.

K8567

Delivered No.209 Sqn 04.02.37; No.240 Sqn 02.03.39; FBTS 05.12.39; Greenock 04.03.41; No.4 OTU 16.03.41. SOC 27.06.41.

K8568

Delivered No.210 Sqn 23.03.37; No.240 Sqn 30.11.38. Hit ground descending out of cloud and forcelanded at Feliwtowe with damaged hull 15.05.39. SOC 08.06.39 as BER.

Four Singapore IIIs delivered to contract 511905/36

K8856

Delivered No.228 Sqn 13.03.37; No.210 Sqn 21.07.37; No.209 Sqn 09.09.38; No.240 Sqn 01.05.39; FBTS date unrecorded. Stalled on landing off Hillhead, Hants, 04.12.39. Sank under tow. SOC 21.01.40.

K8857

Delivered No.209 Sqn 08.04.37. SOC 22.09.39.

K8568 seen derelict at Feliwstowe, stripped of its engines and propellers. It had suffered a landing accident in May 1939, damaging the hull. Considering the cost of repairs, it was left un-repaired and served as stock of spare parts for the remaining Singapores in the UK. (*Phil Jarrett*)

K8858

Delivered No.210 Sqn 27.04.37; No;203 Sqn 06.11.37; Ran aground on reef and wrecked, Hurghada, Red Sea 28.08.39; believed recovered and used as decoy at Aden in June 1940. SOC 12.12.40.

K8859

Delivered No.210 Sqn 09.06.37; No.203 sqn 06.11.37; No.205 Sqn date unrecorded. SOC 20.02.41.

Singapore Mark III, coded '7', believed to be K8856, while serving 210 Sqn in 1937 around the time the squadron was based at Areu (French Algeria). During the last months of that year an Anglo-French force assembled to counter the activities of submarines attacking neutral shipping during the Spanish Civil War. Note the way the undersurfaces of the hull and the floats have been partially painted in black. (*Author's collection*)

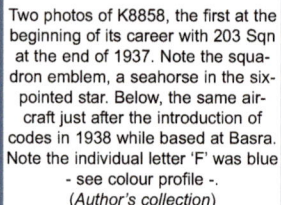

Two photos of K8858, the first at the beginning of its career with 203 Sqn at the end of 1937. Note the squadron emblem, a seahorse in the six-pointed star. Below, the same aircraft just after the introduction of codes in 1938 while based at Basra. Note the individual letter 'F' was blue - see colour profile -.
(*Author's collection*)

Last Singapore to be built, K8859, is seen here before being taken on charge by 210 Sqn in June 1937. It eventually ended its career in Singapore in February 1941, being struck off charge on the 20th, probably for having reached its airframe time-expired limit.
(*Author's collection*)

An impressive photo of three Singapores of 209 Sqn in 1937. K6914/C is leading, followed by K8557/M and K6919/Y, while en route to Malta for the anti-piracy mission the squadron carried out during the last three month of that year. (*Author's collection*)

Singapore Mark III, coded '6' of 205 Squadron based at Seletar, in flight below a formation of Vickers Vildebeests of 100 Squadron, in 1936. The photo doesn't allow clear identification of the Singapore involved. (*Author's collection*)

Roll of Honour
(MILITARY ONLY)

Short Singapore

Name	Rank	Origin	Date	Serial
ALLEN, Cyril Norton	LAC	RAF	15.02.35	K3595
BAILEY, Stephen Thomas	Cpl	RAF	15.02.35	K3595
BEATTY, Henry Longfield	F/L	RAF	15.02.35	K3595
BLAIR, Robert Douglas	P/O	RAF	02.02.37	K3594
FORBES, John Alexander Charles	F/O	RAF	15.02.35	K3595
REES, Roland Dennis James	LAC	RAF	15.02.35	K3595
SCOTT, William Halliburton	AC1	RAF	08.08.39	K4584
SHAW, Alfred Albert	AC1	RAF	10.08.39	K4584
STEED, Leonard Clunie	Sgt	(NZ)/RAF	08.08.39	K4584
WALLACE, William Patrick	LAC	RAF	15.02.35	K3595
WILLIS, Herbert James	Sgt	RAF	15.02.35	K3595
WOGAN, Leslie	AC1	RAF	15.02.35	K3595

Total: 12

Short Singapore Mk.III K3592, No.205 Sqn, Seletar (Singapore), 1936.
The camouflage and marking of the first years of the Singapores were rather simple with only the RAF roundels in the six standard positions, and the serial painted on the rudder, repeated under the wings in opposite directions (see photo 24). 205 Sqn used a non-standard code to identify its Singapores inside the squadron, the symbols of the four card suits, K3592 getting a black Club - see photo p.19.

Short Singapore Mk.III K3593, No.205 Sqn, Seletar (Singapore), 1936.
See K3592 caption for more details and photo p.19.

Short Singapore Mk.III K3593, No.210 Sqn, Pembroke Dock, 1935
See K3592 caption for more details and photo p.19.
The presence of a Seahorse and the inscription '*Occidens Oriensque*' below the cockpit suggests that K3593 was used by 203 Sqn (the seahorse being the symbol of this unit), something never officially sanctioned. The presence of such a drawing is not explained, and can be only provisional and applied during the ferry flight to the Far East for delivery to 205 Sqn while making a stop-over in the Middle east where 203 Sqn was stationed.

Short Singapore Mk.III K3594, No.205 Sqn, Seletar (Singapore), 1936.
See K3592 caption for more details and photo p.20.

Short Singapore Mk.III K4578 No.230 Sqn, Alexandria (Egypt), 1935.
See caption for K3592 for details of the camouflage and markings. 230 Sqn choose numerals to identify its Singapores inside the squadron.

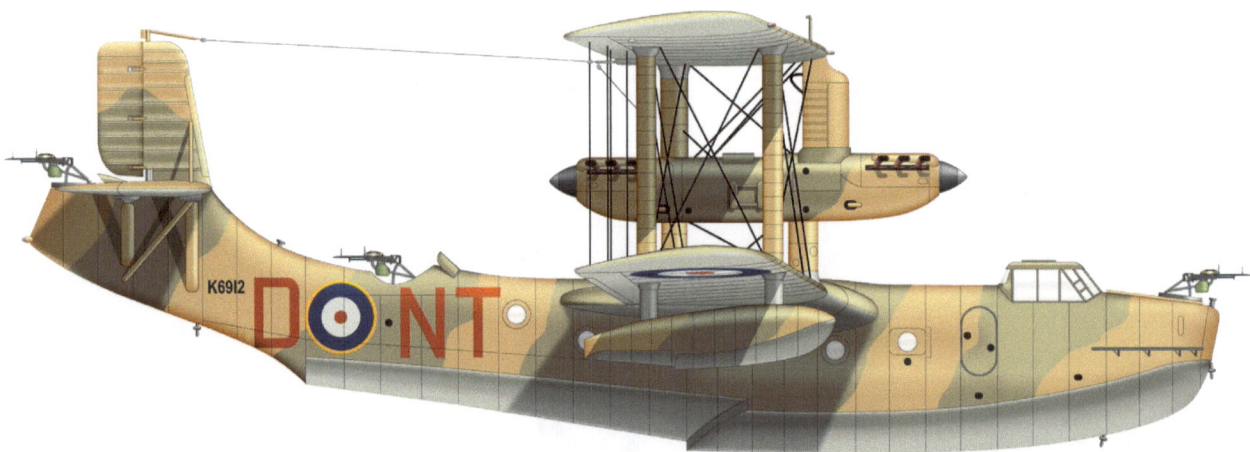

Short Singapore Mk.III K6912, No.203 Sqn, Basra (Iraq), end 1938-1939.
After the Munich crisis, the RAF began to camouflage its aircraft, including flying boats, and assigned squadron codes letters. 203 Sqn stationed at Basra was assigned the letters 'NT'. The photo p.9 suggests the use of non-standard colours for a flying-boat, a camouflage adapted for the desert close to the one used by Blenheims at that time, hence the representation of K6912 painted with Light Earth/Middle Stone and Sky Grey.

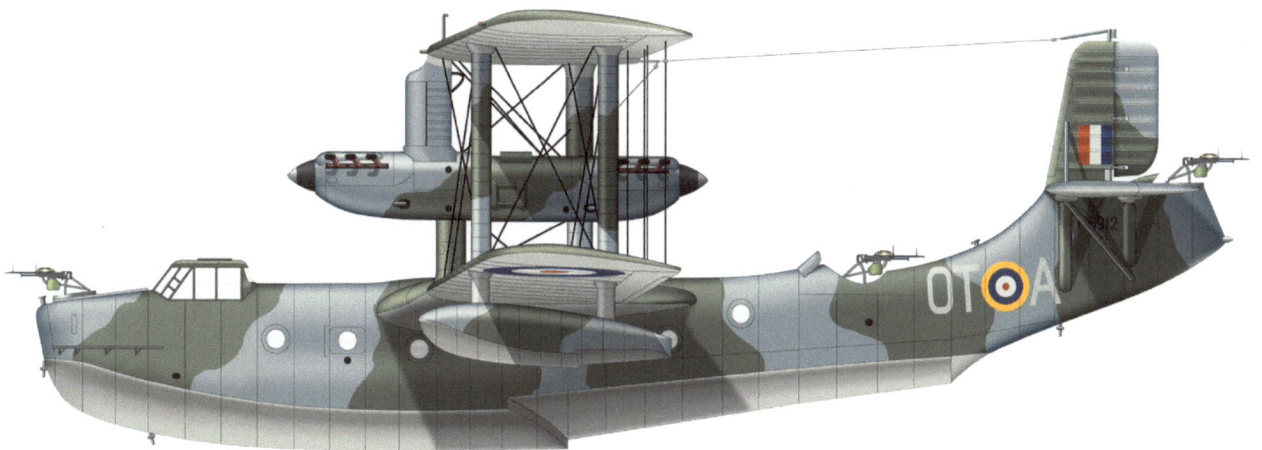

Short Singapore Mk.III K6912, No.5 Sqn, RNZAF, Fiji, end 1941.
The camouflage of the Singapores of the RNZAF seems to have been inherited from the RAF without any change. So it is believed that they were painted faded Extra Dark Sea Grey/faded Dark Slate Grey and Sky Grey for the undersurfaces. It is known that at least one Singapore had its undersides partially repainted in black later in 1942. (see photo p.14 & 26)

Short Singapore Mk.III K6913, No.203 Sqn, Basra (Iraq), 1938.
After having left their Singapores in Natural Metal Finish, the flying-boats began to have a part of their hull and floats painted in Night black. Otherwise, the markings remained basic, except the introduction of the Squadron's Seahorse painted under the cockpit in the white six-pointed stars, black outlined (or possibly blue outlined). (see photo p.26)

Short Singapore Mk.III K6918, No.205 Sqn, Seletar (Singapore), Spring 1941.
By 1940, the aircraft stationed overseas and especially in the Far East began to receive camouflage paint. The photo p.28 suggest a strong contrast inside the colour schemes, meaning that the colours could be Extra Dark Sea Grey/Dark Slate Grey and Sky Grey/Black Night for the undersurfaces, or partially left in natural metal finish.

Short Singapore Mk.III K6921, No.209 Sqn, Mountbatten, September 1937.
See K3592 for details on markings. 209 Sqn was using individual letter to identify their aircraft inside the squadron.

Short Singapore Mk.III K8565, No.4 (C) OTU, Stranraer, 1940/1941.
Photo p.30 shows this aircraft during a training flight over the sea around the end of 1940, beginning of 1941. It is believed to be painted with faded Dark Sea Grey/faded Dark Slate Grey with black undersurfaces, without the roundels on these surfaces as far as it can be seen. However, the three parts of the tail have received extra large fin flashes.

Short Singapore Mk.III K8858, No.203 Sqn, Basra (Iraq), 1938.
This Singapore (see photo p.32) is seen after the introduction of codes in 1938 while based at Basra, the letters 'PP' having been allotted to the squadron. Note the individual letter 'F' painted in blue and the non-standard fuselage roundel. Note also the squadron's Seahorse painted in a six-pointed star, outlined in blue.

www.ingramcontent.com/pod-product-compliance
Lightning Source LLC
Chambersburg PA
CBHW060759090426
42736CB00002B/88